S

Si

Spanish

3

Important
Spanish Words

Des Meagher
Beverley Roberts

Super Simple Spanish ™

This edition first published in 2014.

ISBN 13 978-0-9552198-9-4

Printed and bound in Spain.

For more information about the
Super Simple Spanish series of books
please see our website:

www.supersimplespanish.com

Contents

Introduction

The Super Simple Spanish series of books is designed to make Spanish as simple as possible.

Super Simple Spanish No 3 Important Words has:

Spanish Vocabulary
Over 1200 important and useful Spanish words grouped together under 65 simple headings.

Spanish Pronunciation
Simple Spanish pronunciation and how word stress is used.

Spain Guide
The highlights of Spain with maps of mainland Spain and the Spanish Islands.

The Authors

We love Spain. We try and visit as often as we can. We've worked in Madrid and Seville and spent a small fortune on books over the years trying to improve our Spanish.

Some Spanish books are good and some are not so good. What all our Spanish books have in common is that they are in a drawer somewhere and we never use them. How does that happen?

We took another look at our Spanish books and the answer became clear. Very few of our Spanish books are simple and none of them are super simple. So, starting with vocabulary, we decided to produce a series of books that really would make Spanish Super Simple.

Super Simple Spanish

Each book in the Super Simple Spanish series gives you simple **Spanish Vocabulary**, simple **Spanish Pronunciation** and our **Spain Guide** highlighting the very best of Spain.

The first 3 books in this series are:

No 1. Similar Words
Over 1200 useful words that are amazingly similar in Spanish and English.

No 2. Essential Words
Over 1200 basic and essential Spanish words grouped together under 75 simple headings.

No 3. Important Words
Over 1200 important Spanish words carefully chosen to expand your Spanish vocabulary.

SPANISH VOCABULARY

Important Spanish Words A-Z

PLEASE NOTE

The Spanish Words section has many Spanish words that end in **o**. Words ending in **o** are usually masculine in Spanish.

There are also many words that end in **a** in Spanish and these words are usually feminine.

Some Spanish words can end in **o** or **a** if they are used in the masculine and the feminine.

For example,

amig**o** = male friend
amig**a** = female friend

camarer**o** = waiter
camarer**a** = waitress

To keep the Spanish Vocabulary section as simple as possible we have used the masculine ending **o** for words that can be used in the masculine and the feminine.

ACCESSORIES

accessories	complementos
handbag	bolso
purse	monedero
wallet	cartera
hat	sombrero
cap	gorro
scarf	bufanda
gloves	guantes
umbrella	paraguas
sunglasses	gafas de sol
fan	abanico
wrap	chal

ANIMALS

animal	animal
bird	ave
fish	pez
cat	gato
dog	perro
horse	caballo
cow	vaca
sheep	oveja
pig	cerdo
goat	cabra
bull	toro
donkey	burro

ANIMALS

deer	ciervo
rabbit	conejo
hare	liebre
squirrel	ardilla
hedgehog	erizo
badger	tejón
otter	nutria
snake	serpiente
lizard	lagarto
frog	rana
rat	rata
mouse	ratón

BAR SNACKS

bar snack	tapa
full portion	ración
half portion	media ración
sandwich	sándwich
small roll	montadito
large roll	bocadillo
ham	jamón
cheese	queso
pork loin	lomo
spicy sausage	chorizo
almonds	almendras
olives	aceitunas

BAR SNACKS

Spanish omelette	tortilla de patatas
Russian salad	ensaladilla rusa
croquettes	croquetas
meatballs	albóndigas
prawns	gambas
squid	calamares
fresh anchovies	boquerones
small pasty	empanadilla
tuna pie	empanada de atún
spicy potatoes	patatas bravas
garlic mayo. potatoes	patatas alioli

BEER

beer	cerveza
draught beer	cerveza de barril
small beer	caña
large beer	caña grande
pint	pinta
jug	jarra
shandy	clara / shandy
dark beer	cerveza negra
wheat beer	cerveza de trigo
bottle	botella
can	lata
non-alcoholic	sin alcohol

BIRDS

bird	ave
small bird	pájaro
sparrow	gorrión
robin	petirrojo
swift	vencejo
swallow	golondrina
house martin	avión
blue tit	herrerillo
chaffinch	pinzón
wagtail	lavandera
blackbird	mirlo
pigeon / dove	paloma

BIRDS

magpie	urraca
crow	cuervo
seagull	gaviota
eagle	águila
owl	búho
kestrel	cernícalo
heron	garza
stork	cigüeña
flamingo	flamenco
duck	pato
goose	ganso / oca
swan	cisne

BREAD

bread	pan
baker's	panadería
French stick	barra de pan
white bread	pan blanco
wholemeal	pan integral
rye bread	pan de centeno
sliced bread	pan de molde
baguette	baguette
bread roll	panecillo
toast	tostada
slice of bread	rebanada
breadcrumbs	pan rallado

BUS & TRAIN STATION

bus station	estación de autobuses
train station	estación de trenes
information	información
timetable	horario
destination	destino
arrivals	llegadas
departures	salidas
ticket office	taquilla
ticket	billete
single ticket	ida
return ticket	ida y vuelta

BUS & TRAIN STATION

left-luggage	consigna
platform	andén
train track	vía
taxi rank	parada de taxi
bus stop	parada de autobús
underground	metro
tourist office	oficina de turismo
town map	plano
toilets	servicios lavabos aseos

CAR

car	coche
car key	llave de coche
registration	matrícula
seat belt	cinturón
door	puerta
mirror	retrovisor
indicator	intermitente
lights	luces
headlights	faros
windscreen	parabrisas
w.wipers	limpiaparabrisas
bonnet	capó

CAR

brake	freno
handbrake	freno de mano
accelerator	acelerador
clutch	embrague
tyre	neumático
puncture	pinchazo
wheel	rueda
spare wheel	rueda de recambio
jack	gato
bumper	parachoques
boot	maletero

CAR REPAIR

garage	taller
breakdown	avería
tow truck	grúa
crash	choque
bodywork & respray	chapa y pintura
engine	motor
ignition	encendido
battery	batería
exhaust	tubo de escape
gearbox	caja de cambios
clutch	embrague

14

CAR REPAIR

brake	freno
starter motor	motor de arranque
spark plug	bujía
shock absorber	amortiguador
carburettor	carburador
radiator	radiador
radiator hose	manguito
oil change	cambio de aceite
service	revisión
MOT	ITV
spare part	repuesto

CHEESE

cheese	queso
goat's cheese	queso de cabra
sheep's cheese	queso de oveja
blue cheese	queso azul
cottage cheese	requesón
cream cheese	queso para untar
mature cheese	queso curado
mild cheese	queso tierno
grated cheese	queso rallado
slice	loncha
cheeseboard	tabla de quesos

CITIES

city / town	ciudad
Athens	Atenas
Basle	Basilea
Berne	Berna
Brussels	Bruselas
Cape Town	Ciudad del Cabo
Copenhagen	Copenhague
Edinburgh	Edimburgo
Geneva	Ginebra
The Hague	La Haya
Havana	La Habana
Istanbul	Estambul

CITIES

Lisbon	Lisboa
London	Londres
Moscow	Moscú
New York	Nueva York
Prague	Praga
Rome	Roma
Seoul	Seúl
Stockholm	Estocolmo
Strasbourg	Estrasburgo
Tangiers	Tánger
Vienna	Viena
Warsaw	Varsovia

CITY CENTRE

city / town	ciudad
city centre	centro ciudad
main square	plaza mayor
museum	museo
palace	palacio
cathedral	catedral
castle	castillo
church	iglesia
park	parque
river	río
bridge	puente
stadium	estadio

COFFEE

coffee	café
white coffee	café con leche
black coffee	café americano
coffee with a little milk	café cortado
espresso	café solo
cappuccino	capuchino
coffee & brandy	carajillo
Irish coffee	café irlandés
ground coffee	café molido
instant coffee	café soluble
decaffeinated	descafeinado

COLOURS

colour	color
red	rojo
blue	azul
green	verde
yellow	amarillo
orange	naranja
pink	rosa
purple	morado
black	negro
white	blanco
grey	gris
brown	marrón

COLOURS

beige	beige / beis
khaki	caqui
cream	color crema
multicoloured	multicolor
shade	tono
bright red	rojo fuerte
dark red	rojo oscuro
deep blue	azul intenso
light blue	azul claro
pale green	verde pálido
electric green	verde eléctrico
metallic grey	gris metálico

COUNTRYSIDE

countryside	campo
landscape	paisaje
view	vista
river	río
stream	arroyo
lake	lago
waterfall	cascada
hill	colina
valley	valle
gully	barranco
mountain	montaña
mountain range	sierra

COUNTRYSIDE

reservoir	embalse
wood / forest	bosque
path / track	camino
route	ruta
farm	granja
farmyard	corral
field	campo
meadow	prado
livestock	ganado
vineyard	viñedo
wildlife	fauna y flora
nature	naturaleza

DAY

day	día
morning	mañana
afternoon	tarde
evening	tarde
night	noche
midday	mediodía
midnight	medianoche
early morning	madrugada
dawn	amanecer
dusk	anochecer
sunrise	salida del sol
sunset	puesta del sol

DENTIST'S

dentist	dentista
appointment	cita / hora
check-up	revisión
pain	dolor
tooth	diente
gum	encía
filling	empaste
bridge	puente
crown	corona
extraction	extracción
dentures	dentadura postiza

DIY

DIY	bricolaje
ironmonger's	ferretería
tools	herramientas
screwdriver	destornillador
drill	taladro
hammer	martillo
saw	sierra
pliers	alicates
spanner	llave
Stanley knife®	cuchilla cútter®
spirit level	nivel de burbuja

DIY

ladder	escalera de mano
paint	pintura
paintbrush	brocha
roller	rodillo
turpentine	aguarrás
nail	clavo
screw	tornillo
hook	gancho
Rawlplug®	taco de plástico
nut	tuerca
bolt	perno
washer	arandela

DIY

wall tile	azulejo
floor tile	baldosa
grout	lechada
sealant	sellador
sand	arena
gravel	grava
cement	cemento
concrete	hormigón
brick	ladrillo
wood	madera
glass	cristal
plaster	yeso

EATING OUT

menu	carta
set menu	menú del día
wine list	carta de vinos
cutlery	cubiertos
knife	cuchillo
fork	tenedor
spoon	cuchara
glass	vaso
plate	plato
serviette	servilleta
still water	agua sin gas
sparkling water	agua con gas

EATING OUT

wine	vino
beer	cerveza
soft drink	refresco
juice	zumo
salt	sal
pepper	pimienta
ketchup	ketchup
mayonnaise	mahonesa
mustard	mostaza
oil	aceite
vinegar	vinagre
bill	cuenta

FABRICS

fabric	tela
cotton	algodón
linen	lino
satin	satén
silk	seda
wool	lana
cashmere	cachemir
leather	piel
nylon	nylon
polyester	poliéster
plain	liso
patterned	estampado

FISH

fish	pescado
fishmonger's	pescadería
sardines	sardinas
salmon	salmón
tuna	atún / bonito
cod	bacalao
hake	merluza
red mullet	salmonete
monkfish	rape
swordfish	emperador / pez espada
mackerel	caballa

FISH

sole	lenguado
sea bass	lubina
red bream	besugo
gilthead bream	dorada
turbot	rodaballo
trout	trucha
anchovies	boquerones
salted anchovies	anchoas
whitebait	chanquetes
whiting	pescadilla
fish roe	huevas
salted fish	salazones

FLAVOURS

flavour	sabor
strong	fuerte
mild	suave
spicy	picante
curried	al curry
sweet	dulce
sour	agrio
bitter	amargo
dry	seco
salty	salado
peppery	a pimienta
creamy	cremoso

FLOWERS

flowers	flores
florist's	floristería
vase	florero
bouquet	ramo
rose	rosa
carnation	clavel
chrysanthemum	crisantemo
daffodil	narciso
tulip	tulipán
iris	lirio
lily	azucena
freesia	fresia

FLOWERS

sunflower	girasol
marigold	maravilla
violet	violeta
pansy	pensamiento
daisy	margarita
orchid	orquídea
geranium	geranio
begonia	begonia
hibiscus	hibisco
bougainvillea	buganvilla
plant	planta
plant pot	maceta

FOOTBALL

football	fútbol
player	jugador
manager	entrenador
team	equipo
goalkeeper	portero
defender	defensa
central defender	central
fullback	lateral
midfielder	centrocampista
winger	extremo
forward	delantero
substitute	suplente

FOOTBALL

shot	disparo
save	parada
pass	pase
tackle	entrada
foul	falta
yellow card	tarjeta amarilla
red card	tarjeta roja
referee	árbitro
goal	gol
offside	fuera de juego
stadium	estadio
fans	aficionados

FRUIT

fruit	fruta
apple	manzana
orange	naranja
pear	pera
banana	plátano
grape	uva
melon	melón
watermelon	sandía
pineapple	piña
strawberry	fresa
raspberry	frambuesa
peach	melocotón

FRUIT

apricot	albaricoque
cherry	cereza
lemon	limón
lime	lima
plum	ciruela
pomegranate	granada
fig	higo
blackberry	mora
blueberry	arándano
gooseberry	grosella
blackcurrant	grosella negra
redcurrant	grosella roja

FURNITURE

furniture	muebles
sofa	sofá
sofa bed	sofá cama
armchair	sillón
recliner	sillón reclinable
footstool	escabel
table	mesa
chair	silla
coffee table	mesa de centro
nest of tables	mesa nido
sideboard	aparador
display cabinet	vitrina

FURNITURE

bed	cama
headboard	cabecera
mattress	colchón
single bed	cama individual
double bed	cama doble
bedside table	mesa de noche
dressing table	tocador
chest of drawers	cómoda
wardrobe	armario
garden furniture	muebles de jardín
sunlounger	tumbona
bench	banco

GAMES

game	juego
cards	cartas / naipes
bridge	bridge
poker	póker
dominoes	dominó
draughts	damas
chess	ajedrez
darts	dardos
pool/snooker/ billiards	billar
board game	juego de mesa
video game	videojuego

HERBS

herb	hierba
parsley	perejil
thyme	tomillo
oregano	orégano
rosemary	romero
mint	menta / hierbabuena
bayleaf	laurel
basil	albahaca
sage	salvia
tarragon	estragón
coriander	cilantro

HOUSEHOLD ITEMS

matches	cerillas
lighter	mechero
batteries	pilas
light bulb	bombilla
torch	linterna
scissors	tijeras
tin opener	abrelatas
bottle opener	abrebotellas
corkscrew	sacacorchos
plaster	tirita®
adaptor	adaptador
extension lead	extensión

HOUSEHOLD ITEMS

heater	calentador
fan	ventilador
coat hanger	percha
clothes peg	pinza
clothes airer	tendedero
rubbish bin	cubo de basura
bin liner	bolsa de basura
kitchen roll	rollo de cocina
dustpan	recogedor
brush	cepillo
mop	fregona
adhesive tape	cinta adhesiva

HUMAN BODY

body	cuerpo
brain	cerebro
heart	corazón
lung	pulmón
skin	piel
bone	hueso
head	cabeza
ear	oreja
nose	nariz
throat	garganta
eye	ojo
mouth	boca

HUMAN BODY

lip	labio
tongue	lengua
neck	cuello
shoulder	hombro
back	espalda
spine	columna
chest	pecho
stomach	estómago
waist	cintura
hip	cadera
arm	brazo
elbow	codo

HUMAN BODY

wrist	muñeca
hand	mano
finger	dedo
thumb	pulgar
nail	uña
leg	pierna
knee	rodilla
ankle	tobillo
foot	pie
toe	dedo del pie
big toe	dedo gordo
heel	talón

ICE CREAM

ice cream	helado
ice cream parlour	heladería
flavour	sabor
vanilla	vainilla
chocolate	chocolate
strawberry	fresa
scoop	bola
cone	cucurucho
tub	tarrina
wafer	barquillo
syrup	sirope

IN-LAWS

in-laws	parientes políticos
father-in-law	suegro / padre político
mother-in-law	suegra / madre política
son-in-law	yerno / hijo político
daughter-in-law	nuera / hija política
brother-in-law	cuñado / hermano político
sister-in-law	cuñada / hermana política

LEISURE

leisure	ocio
free time	tiempo libre
cinema	cine
film	película
theatre	teatro
concert	concierto
show	espectáculo
dance	baile
circus	circo
funfair	parque de atracciones
water park	parque acuático

MARITAL STATUS

marital status	estado civil
married	casado
single	soltero
divorced	divorciado
separated	separado
widow	viuda
widower	viudo
husband	marido
wife	esposa
partner	pareja
civil marriage	matrimonio civil

MEALS

meal	comida
breakfast	desayuno
lunch	almuerzo
set menu	menú del día
afternoon tea	merienda
dinner	cena
supper	cena
appetiser	aperitivo
bar snacks	tapas
buffet	buffet
set price buffet	buffet libre

MEAT

meat	carne
beef	ternera
lamb	cordero
pork	cerdo
chicken	pollo
turkey	pavo
duck	pato
rabbit	conejo
goat	cabra
oxtail	rabo de toro
venison	venado
wild boar	jabalí

MEAT

steak	bistec
rare	poco hecho
medium	a punto
well done	muy hecho
sirloin	solomillo
pork loin	lomo
chop	chuleta
breast	pechuga
spare ribs	costillas
leg	pierna
wing	alita
thigh	muslo

MEAT

bacon	bacon
sausage	salchicha
meatballs	albóndigas
liver	hígado
kidneys	riñones
black pudding	morcilla
pie	empanada
small pasty	empanadilla
mince	carne picada
lean meat	carne magra
stewing steak	carne para estofar

MUSIC

music	música
live music	música en vivo
musician	músico
song	canción
songwriter	compositor
singer	cantante
group	grupo
band	banda
orchestra	orquesta
choir	coro
concert	concierto
tour	gira

MUSIC

musical instrument	instrumento musical
guitar	guitarra
electric guitar	guitarra eléctrica
Spanish guitar	guitarra española
piano	piano
violin	violín
saxophone	saxofón
trumpet	trompeta
clarinet	clarinete
flute	flauta
drums	batería

NATIONALITIES

nationality	nacionalidad
British	británico
English	inglés
Scottish	escocés
Welsh	galés
Northern Irish	norirlandés
Irish	irlandés
Spanish	español
Portuguese	portugués
French	francés
German	alemán
Italian	italiano

NATIONALITIES

Dutch	holandés
Belgian	belga
Swiss	suizo
Danish	danés
Swedish	sueco
Norwegian	noruego
Finnish	finlandés
American	estadounidense
Canadian	canadiense
Russian	ruso
Chinese	chino
Japanese	japonés

NUMBERS

number	número
zero	cero
one	uno
two	dos
three	tres
four	cuatro
five	cinco
six	seis
seven	siete
eight	ocho
nine	nueve
ten	diez

NUMBERS

first	primero
last	último
second	segundo
third	tercero
fourth	cuarto
fifth	quinto
sixth	sexto
seventh	séptimo
eighth	octavo
ninth	noveno
tenth	décimo
eleventh	undécimo

NUTS

nuts	frutos secos
peanut	cacahuete
almond	almendra
pistachio	pistacho
cashew	anacardo
walnut	nuez
pecan	pacana
pine nut	piñón
chestnut	castaña
hazlenut	avellana
Brazil nut	nuez de Brasil
coconut	coco

OPTICIAN'S

optician's	óptica
eye	ojo
eye test	examen de ojos
appointment	cita / hora
glasses	gafas
sunglasses	gafas de sol
glasses case	estuche
frame	montura
lens	cristal
contact lens	lentilla
short-sighted	miope
long-sighted	hipermétrope

PETROL STATION

petrol station	gasolinera
petrol	gasolina
unleaded	sin plomo
diesel	diesel / gasóleo
oil	aceite
air	aire
water	agua
tyre	neumático
pressure	presión
carwash	lavado
car vacuum	aspiradora
shop	tienda

PETS

pet	mascota
dog	perro
bitch	perra
puppy	cachorro
cat	gato
female cat	gata
kitten	gatito
coat	pelaje
fur	pelaje
tail	cola
paw	pata
claw	uña

PETS

collar	collar
lead	correa
microchip	microchip
rabbit	conejo
hamster	hámster
gerbil	jerbo
guinea pig	cobayo
tortoise	tortuga
male	macho
female	hembra
breed	raza
vet	veterinario

PORT

port	puerto
boat	barco
fishing boat	barco de pesca
yacht	yate
cruise ship	crucero
ferry	ferry
customs	aduana
quay	muelle
fish market	lonja
yacht club	club náutico
marina	puerto deportivo

PROFESSIONS

profession	profesión
doctor	médico
dentist	dentista
optician	óptico
pharmacist	farmacéutico
vet	veterinario
architect	arquitecto
engineer	ingeniero
accountant	contable
lawyer	abogado
notary	notario
teacher	profesor

READING

bookshop	librería
library	biblioteca
kiosk	kiosco
the press	prensa
newspaper	periódico
magazine	revista
comic	tebeo
book	libro
eBook	eBook
fiction	ficción
non-fiction	no ficción
bestseller	bestseller

READING

novel	novela
novelist	novelista
paperback	tapa blanda
hardback	tapa dura
biography	biografía
autobiography	autobiografía
guidebook	guía
manual	manual
dictionary	diccionario
map	mapa
atlas	atlas
brochure	folleto

SALAD

salad	ensalada
lettuce	lechuga
lettuce heart	cogollo
rocket	rúcula
tomato	tomate
onion	cebolla
cucumber	pepino
celery	apio
beetroot	remolacha
radish	rábano
green olives	aceitunas verdes
black olives	aceitunas negras

SALAD

carrot	zanahoria
spring onion	cebollana
green pepper	pimiento verde
red pepper	pimiento rojo
asparagus	espárrago
avocado	aguacate
palm heart	palmito
sweetcorn	maíz dulce
gherkin	pepinillo
capers	alcaparras
cocktail onion	cebollita perla
salad dressing	aliño

SAUCES

sauce	salsa
ketchup	ketchup
mustard	mostaza
mayonnaise	mahonesa
barbecue sauce	salsa barbacoa
sweet & sour s.	salsa agridulce
cocktail sauce	salsa rosa
soya sauce	salsa de soja
tartare sauce	salsa tártara
spicy tomato s.	salsa brava
garlic mayonnaise	alioli

SCHOOL

school	colegio
teacher	profesor
pupil	alumno
class	clase
classroom	aula
timetable	horario
course	curso
term	trimestre
textbook	libro de texto
homework	deberes
revision	repaso
exam	examen

SEA

sea	mar
sea view	vista al mar
seafront	paseo marítimo
seashore	orilla del mar
beach	playa
sand	arena
seashell	concha
wave	ola
tide	marea
high tide	marea alta
low tide	marea baja
current	corriente

SEA

coastline	costa
cape	cabo
lighthouse	faro
rock	roca
reef	arrecife
coral reef	arrecife de coral
island	isla
bay	bahía
cove	cala
sea breeze	brisa marina
sea mist	bruma
rough sea	mar gruesa

SEAFOOD

seafood	mariscos
seafood platter	mariscada
prawns	gambas
king prawn	langostino
lobster	langosta / bogavante
crayfish	cigala
scallops	vieiras
oyster	ostra
mussels	mejillones
clams	almejas
crab	cangrejo

SEAFOOD

octopus	pulpo
squid	calamares
small squid	chipirones
baby squid	chopitos
cuttlefish	sepia
cockles	berberechos
shrimp	camarones
razor clam	navaja
seafood soup	sopa de marisco
seafood restaurant	marisquería

SHOPS

shop	tienda
baker's	panadería
greengrocer's	frutería
butcher's	carnicería
fishmonger's	pescadería
tobacconist's	tabacos
wine merchant	bodega
chemist's	farmacia
post office	Correos
ironmonger's	ferretería
dry cleaner's	tintorería
launderette	lavandería

SHOPS

jeweller's	joyería
watchmaker's	relojería
shoe shop	zapatería
footwear	calzado
bookshop	librería
stationer's	papelería
gifts	regalos
accessories	complementos
lingerie	lencería
costume jewellery	bisutería
ceramics	cerámica

SPICES

spice	especia
spicy	picante
pepper	pimienta
paprika	pimentón
cayenne	cayena
garlic	ajo
cloves	clavo
saffron	azafrán
cumin	comino
ginger	jengibre
cinnamon	canela
nutmeg	nuez moscada

SPORT

sport	deporte
football	fútbol
rugby	rugby
cricket	críquet
basketball	baloncesto
golf	golf
tennis	tenis
hockey	hockey
athletics	atletismo
cycling	ciclismo
swimming	natación
gymnastics	gimnasia

SPORT

baseball	béisbol
volleyball	vóleibol
handball	balonmano
badminton	bádminton
squash	squash
boxing	boxeo
judo	judo
horse racing	turf
sailing	vela
motor sport	automovilismo
motorbike racing	motociclismo

SWIMMING

swimming	natación
swimming pool	piscina
lifeguard	socorrista
changing room	vestuario
swimwear	bañadores
cap	gorro de baño
goggles	gafas de natación
face mask	máscara
float	flotador
shower	ducha
towel	toalla

TEA

tea	té
milk	leche
sugar	azúcar
tea bag	bolsita de té
tea leaves	hojas de té
teapot	tetera
cup	taza
green tea	té verde
red tea	té rojo
herbal tea	infusión
mint tea	menta poleo
camomile tea	manzanilla

TELEVISION

television	televisión
television set	televisor
picture	imagen
screen	pantalla
signal	señal
digital	digital
satellite	satélite
satellite dish	parabólica
aerial	antena
cable	cable
remote control	mando a distancia

TELEVISION

channel	canal
teletext	teletexto
programme	programa
news	noticias
sport	deporte
weather	tiempo
documentary	documental
soap opera	telenovela
series	serie
film	película
subtitle	subtítulo
advert	anuncio

TOYS

toy	juguete
soft toy	peluche
teddy bear	oso de peluche
doll	muñeca
bat	bate
ball	balón / pelota
skates	patines
scooter	patinete
skateboard	monopatín
bike	bici
game	juego
present	regalo

TREES

tree	árbol
wood / forest	bosque
palm tree	palmera
pine	pino
oak	roble
elm	olmo
maple	arce
lime	tilo
chestnut	castaño
eucalyptus	eucalipto
beech	haya
birch	abedul

TREES

fruit tree	frutal
orchard	huerta
olive tree	olivo
orange tree	naranjo
lemon tree	limonero
lime tree	limero
cherry tree	cerezo
almond tree	almendro
apple tree	manzano
plum tree	ciruelo
pear tree	peral
fig tree	higuera

VEGETABLES

vegetables	verduras
potato	patata
carrot	zanahoria
onion	cebolla
cauliflower	coliflor
cabbage	col
peas	guisantes
green beans	judías verdes
spinach	espinaca
broccoli	brócoli
leek	puerro
asparagus	espárrago

VEGETABLES

aubergine	berenjena
marrow	calabaza
courgette	calabacín
artichoke	alcachofa
red cabbage	col lombarda
Swiss chard	acelgas
turnip	nabo
swede	nabo sueco
parsnip	chirivía
Brussels sprout	col de Bruselas
sweetcorn	maíz dulce
mushrooms	champiñones

WEATHER

weather	tiempo
forecast	pronóstico
sun	sol
sunny	soleado
hot	caluroso / cálido
muggy	bochorno
cloud	nube
cloudy	nuboso
cool	fresco
cold	frío
very cold	helado

WEATHER

breeze	brisa
wind	viento
gust of wind	racha
rain	lluvia
shower	chubasco
storm	tormenta
thunder	truenos
lightning	rayo
fog	niebla
mist	neblina
hail	granizo
snow	nieve

WEIGHTS & MEASURES

dimensions	dimensiones
height	altura
width	anchura
depth	profundidad
length	longitud
millimetre	milímetro
centimetre	centímetro
metre	metro
kilometre	kilómetro
square metre	metro cuadrado
mile	milla
nautical mile	milla náutica

WEIGHTS & MEASURES

weight	peso
milligram	miligramo
centigram	centigramo
gram	gramo
kilogram	kilogramo
half kilo	medio kilo
quarter kilo	cuarto kilo
liquid	líquido
millilitre	mililitro
centilitre	centilitro
litre	litro
measurement	medida

WILD ANIMALS

wild animal	animal salvaje
lion	león
tiger	tigre
leopard	leopardo
cheetah	chita
jaguar	jaguar
elephant	elefante
rhinoceros	rinoceronte
hippopotamus	hipopótamo
giraffe	jirafa
antelope	antílope
zebra	cebra

WILD ANIMALS

buffalo	búfalo
hyena	hiena
crocodile	cocodrilo
alligator	aligátor
gorilla	gorila
monkey	mono
chimpanzee	chimpancé
bear	oso
wolf	lobo
fox	zorro
wild boar	jabalí
lynx	lince

WINE

wine	vino
glass of wine	copa de vino
bottle of wine	botella de vino
red wine	vino tinto
white wine	vino blanco
rosé wine	vino rosado
sparkling wine	cava
champagne	champán
sweet	dulce
dry	seco
red wine & lemonade	tinto de verano

WORK

work / job	trabajo
employment	empleo
employer	empleador
employee	empleado
self-employed	autónomo
full-time	tiempo completo
part-time	tiempo parcial
boss	jefe
manager	gerente
colleague	colega
salary	salario
shift	turno

WORK

civil servant	funcionario
secretary	secretario
administrator	administrador
receptionist	recepcionista
shop assistant	dependiente
nurse	enfermero
social worker	asistente social
hairdresser	peluquero
cook	cocinero
waiter	camarero
cleaner	limpiador
taxi driver	taxista

WORK

police officer	agente de policía
firefighter	bombero
bus driver	chófer
mechanic	mecánico
builder	albañil
electrician	electricista
plumber	fontanero
carpenter	carpintero
locksmith	cerrajero
glazier	cristalero
painter	pintor

WORLD

world	mundo
ocean	océano
land	tierra
sea	mar
sky	cielo
region	región
country	país
continent	continente
equator	ecuador
rainforest	selva tropical
desert	desierto
climate	clima

Spanish Pronunciation

Pronunciation

Pronunciation Summary

Spanish Word Stress

Spanish Pronunciation

■ ce

In Spanish ce is pronounced like the th in thanks.

Practise saying this th sound with these Spanish words:

cerca	near
cero	zero
cerdo	pig
centro	centre
cesta	basket

Spanish Pronunciation

▪ ci

In Spanish ci is pronounced like the th in thanks.

Practise saying this th sound with these Spanish words.

cinco	five
cita	appointment
cien	one hundred
circo	circus
circular	circular

Spanish Pronunciation

▪ e

In Spanish e at the end of a word is pronounced like a – the first letter of the English alphabet.

Practise saying this a sound with these Spanish words.

madre	mother
padre	father
coche	car
leche	milk
grande	big

Spanish Pronunciation

▪ ge

In Spanish ge is pronounced like the ch in the Scottish word loch. This is a back-of-the-throat sound as if clearing the throat!

Practise saying this throaty loch sound with these Spanish words.

general	general
generoso	generous
genial	brilliant
gente	people
gel	gel

Spanish Pronunciation

▪ gi

In Spanish gi is pronounced like the ch in the Scottish word loch. This is a back-of-the-throat sound as if clearing the throat!

Practise saying this throaty loch sound with these Spanish words.

ginebra	gin
gimnasta	gymnast
gimnasio	gym
gitano	gypsy
gira	tour

Spanish Pronunciation

▪ h

In Spanish h has no sound.
It is a silent letter.

Practise saying these Spanish
words making sure h has no
sound.

hola	hello
hora	hour
hoy	today
hombre	man
hospital	hospital

Spanish Pronunciation

▪ j

In Spanish j is pronounced like the ch in the Scottish word loch. This is a back-of-the throat sound as if clearing the throat!

Practise saying this throaty loch sound with these Spanish words.

jamón	ham
jardín	garden
jarra	jug
junio	June
julio	July

Spanish Pronunciation

▪ ll

In Spanish ll is pronounced like the y in yes.

Practise saying this y sound with these Spanish words.

tortilla	omelette
castillo	castle
cuchillo	knife
botella	bottle
caballo	horse

Spanish Pronunciation

■ ñ

In Spanish ñ is pronounced like ny in canyon.

Practise saying this ny sound with these Spanish words.

España	Spain
mañana	tomorrow
montaña	mountain
piña	pineapple
Señorita	Miss

Spanish Pronunciation

■ V

In Spanish v at the beginning of a word is pronounced like b in big.

Practise saying this b sound with these Spanish words.

vino	wine
verano	summer
verde	green
vaso	glass
vale	okay

Spanish Pronunciation

▪ Z

In Spanish z is pronounced like the th in thanks.

Practise saying this th sound with these Spanish words.

zumo	juice
zapato	shoe
zona	area
plaza	square
taza	cup

Spanish Pronunciation

Summary

ce, ci and z is th in thanks

e at the end of a word is a – the sound of the first letter of the English alphabet.

ge, gi and j is ch in loch

h is silent

ll is y in yes

ñ is ny in canyon

v at the start of a word is b in big

Spanish Pronunciation

Word Stress

Spanish words are normally stressed on the last syllable.

actor normal papel popular

But if a Spanish word ends in a, e, i, o, u, s or n the stress is on the last-but-one syllable.

nota arte plato intenso

If a Spanish word has an accent (′) the stress is on the accent.

bebé melón adiós teléfono

SPAIN GUIDE

The Highlights of Spain

Maps of Mainland Spain and the Spanish Islands

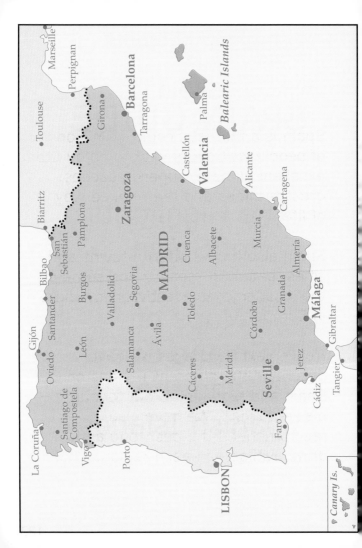

Spain

Spain is a fantastic country. Millions of people visit every year to enjoy the excellent climate, superb beaches, great facilities and the relaxed way of life.

Spain also has wonderful towns and cities, beautiful scenery and some of the most enjoyable festivals anywhere in Europe.

In the next few pages we have described the different regions of Spain and highlighted our favourite places to visit. We have also recommended the best food and drink available in each region.

Southern Spain

Andalucía covers all of southern Spain and runs for over 350 miles from the Portuguese border in the west to the province of Almería in the east. Andalucía is a beautiful and popular region of Spain.

There are excellent beaches all along the coastline. The best beaches are on the Atlantic coast of the Costa de la Luz and along the Mediterranean coast of Almería. Inland there are dramatic mountain ranges and beautiful landscapes.

The cities of Granada, Córdoba and Seville have some of the most interesting and important monuments in Europe and are great places to visit. Andalucía is also famous for some of the most colourful and exciting festivals held in Spain.

Highlights of Southern Spain

Places to Visit

Granada's Alhambra palace and gardens. Córdoba's Mezquita mosque and the old town. Seville's Alcázar palace and gardens, Giralda tower and old town. The attractive towns and cities of Cádiz, Jerez and Ronda.

Food and Drink

chilled soups	gazpacho & salmorejo
fried fish	fritura de pescado
cured ham	jamón ibérico
bar snacks	tapas
draught beer	caña
dry sherry	fino & manzanilla
fruit punch	sangría
red wine & lemonade	tinto de verano

Eastern Spain

Eastern Spain consists of the regions of Cataluña, Valencia and Murcia. This large region stretches for over 500 miles from the French border in the north to Andalucía in the south.

This region has some of the best scenery in Spain. The Costa Brava, the area around Dénia and the Mar Menor are exceptionally beautiful. The east coast is home to some of the best known holiday resorts in Spain attracting millions of visitors because of the excellent climate, great beaches and superb facilities.

Barcelona is the cultural and commercial capital of Cataluña and one of the best cities in Europe. Valencia and Murcia are also important and attractive regional capitals.

Highlights of Eastern Spain

Places to Visit

Barcelona's Sagrada Familia cathedral, Gaudi's buildings and Park Güell, the old town and La Rambla. Valencia's historic centre and City of Arts and Sciences. Alicante's beach, seafront and marina. The attractive centres of Gerona, Murcia, Elche and Cartagena.

Food and Drink

paella & rice dishes	arroces
shellfish & noodles	fideuá
Catalan sausage	butifarra
fresh salad	ensalada
fresh fruit	fruta del tiempo

sparkling wine	cava
white wines	Penedés region
red wines	Priorato region
rosé wines	Ampurdán

Northern Spain

Northern Spain includes the regions of Galicia, Asturias, Cantabria, the Basque Country and Navarra. It runs for 350 miles from the Atlantic in the west to the Pyrenees in the east. This area has a cooler and wetter climate than the rest of the country and is sometimes called "Green Spain".

The coastline of Galicia is especially beautiful and there are excellent beaches all along the north coast. The mountains of the Picos de Europa and the Spanish Pyrenees have some of the best scenery in Spain.

This region hosts the beautiful resorts of San Sebastián and Santander and the attractive cities of Santiago de Compostela, Oviedo and La Coruña. Bilbao is home to the fantastic Guggenheim Museum.

Highlights of Northern Spain

Places to Visit

Santiago de Compostela's **cathedral and old town.** San Sebastián's **bay, beaches and headlands.** Santander's **bays and beaches.** Oviedo's **old town.**

The stunning coastline of Galicia.

Food and Drink

fresh fish	pescados
seafood	mariscos
tuna pie	empanada de atún
bean stew	fabada asturiana
blue cheese	cabrales
white wines	Albariño, Ribeiro, Rías Baixas
cider	sidra
liqueur	orujo

Central Spain

Central Spain covers a huge area from Andalucía in the south to Asturias and Cantabria in the north, from the Portuguese border in the west to Cataluña, Valencia and Murcia in the east. To the south of Madrid there is Castille La Mancha and Extremadura and to the north Castille and León, La Rioja and Aragón.

This massive plain has incredible blue skies throughout the year and is only broken up by mountain ranges to the north and west of Madrid.

Spain's fantastic capital city is in the centre of this region and almost exactly in the centre of Spain. Around Madrid cities like Salamanca, Segovia, Toledo and Ávila are some of the most historic and beautiful cities in Spain.

Highlights of Central Spain

Places to Visit

Madrid's Plaza Mayor, Royal Palace and
the Thyssen, Prado and Reina Sofía
museums. The Retiro Park and gardens.
León's cathedral and old town.
Salamanca's Plaza Mayor and old town.
Ávila's city walls and historic centre.
Segovia's Alcázar and aqueduct.
Toledo's cathedral, historic centre and
El Greco paintings.

Food and Drink

roast lamb	cordero asado
suckling pig	cochinillo asado
ratatouille	pisto manchego
ham	jamón ibérico
cheese	queso manchego
red wines	Rioja, Ribera del Duero
white wines	Rueda, Rioja

The Spanish Islands

Spain has two groups of islands, the Balearic Islands in the Mediterranean and the Canary Islands off the coast of Morocco in the Atlantic.

The Balearic Islands consist of Mallorca, Menorca, Ibiza and Formentera.
The Balearics have stunning coastlines, beautiful coves, excellent beaches and some of the best tourist facilities in Europe. Palma de Mallorca, Ibiza and Mahón are lively and attractive capital cities.

The Canary Islands are Gran Canaria, Lanzarote, Fuerteventura, Tenerife, La Gomera, El Hierro and La Palma.
The Canaries have an excellent year round climate, dramatic volcanic landscapes, some excellent beaches and vibrant capital cities in Las Palmas de Gran Canaria and Santa Cruz de Tenerife.

Highlights of the Islands

Places to Visit

Balearics - Palma, Ibiza, Mahón and Ciutadella. The beaches of northern Mallorca, southern Menorca and Ibiza. Canaries - Las Palmas, Santa Cruz de Tenerife. The beaches of Gran Canaria and Fuerteventura. Volcanic landscapes in Lanzarote and Tenerife.

Food and Drink

Balearics

breakfast pastry	ensaimada
Menorcan cheese	queso de Mahón
local wine	Binissalem

The Canaries

fresh fish	pescados
salted potatoes	papas arrugadas
spicy sauce	mojo colorado
rum	ron

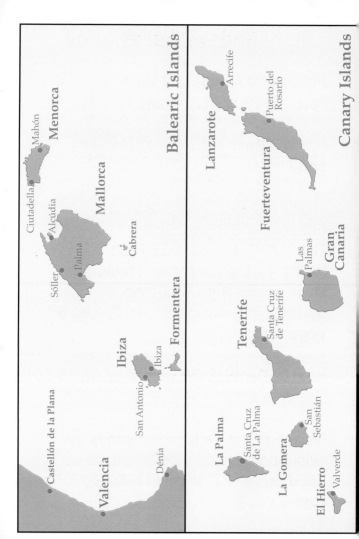

Index-Índice

Index-Índice